RYUHO OKAWA

WHAT WILL BECOME OF CORONAVIRUS PANDEMIC?

READINGS BY EDGAR CAYCE

HS PRESS

Original title: *Corona Pandemic wa Do naru ka*
HS Press is an imprint of IRH Press Co., Ltd.
Tokyo
ISBN 13: 978-1-943869-82-4
ISBN 10: 1-943869-82-0
Cover Image: IgorZh/Gargantiopa/shutterstock.com

Contents

Preface

Now, the coronavirus pandemic is all the media covers.

According to the newspapers this morning, this year's world economic growth is projected at minus 3 percent. But this is assuming that the coronavirus infection will settle in a short time.

What I can do on my part is to share with you the analyses and predictions of the high spirits and beings referred to as gods that are concerned about or involved in the coronavirus pandemic. There may be contradictions due to the difference in character, but the general trend can be predicted.

I'd like you to read Chapters One and Two in particular, but I'd also like you to know their background, so I have attached an appendix.* It is

---

* Translator's note: This book is a translation of Chapter Two of the original Japanese edition. The original edition includes Chapter One, "Coronavirus Pandemic Reading by Kuni-no-Tokotachi-no-Kami" and Appendix, "Spiritual Messages from Kuni-no-Tokotachi-no-Kami" (two sessions) and "Spiritual Messages from Shotoku Taishi."

unfortunate that there is a Japanese god still closed-minded, but it is a relief that Amaterasu-O-Mikami (a great goddess of Japan) is open-minded. The future can still be changed.

Ryuho Okawa
Master & CEO of Happy Science Group
April 15, 2020

What Will Become of Coronavirus Pandemic?

Readings by Edgar Cayce

Originally recorded in Japanese on April 9, 2020,
in the Special Lecture Hall of Happy Science in Japan,
and later translated into English.

Edgar Cayce (1877 - 1945)

An American prophet and spiritual healer, sometimes called, "The Sleeping Prophet" and "The Miracle Man of Virginia Beach." He conducted over 14,000 readings on ways to treat disease, consultations on life, and super-ancient history while being in a hypnotic state. The core spirit of Edgar Cayce's soul is said to be the leader of the healing spirit group, Sariel (one of the Seven Archangels). Refer to *The Nine Dimensions: Unveiling the Laws of Eternity* (New York: IRH Press, 2012).

Interviewers from Happy Science*

Ryo Takeda

Vice Chairperson
Chief Secretary of Religious Affairs Headquarters

Sakurako Jinmu

Managing Director
Chief Secretary, First Secretarial Division
Religious Affairs Headquarters

Masayuki Isono

Executive Director
Chief of Overseas Missionary Work Promotion Office
Deputy Chief Secretary, First Secretarial Division
Religious Affairs Headquarters

The opinions of the spirit do not necessarily reflect those of Happy Science Group.
For the mechanism behind spiritual messages, see the end section.

---

* Interviewers are listed in the order that they appear in the transcript.
Their professional titles represent their positions at the time of the interview.

1

The Surprising Foresight about the Spread of the Novel Coronavirus Infection

Inviting Edgar Cayce and asking him about the world situation

RYUHO OKAWA

Now, I'd like to ask Edgar Cayce, who passed away around the time the war between Japan and its former enemy the United States ended, about whether he shares the same thoughts like the ones we heard just a moment ago*. While Edgar Cayce is technically on the American side, at Happy Science, I have discussions with him and Gyoki (a Japanese Buddhist monk, 668-749 AD) on a day-to-day basis regarding specific details about managing the organization. Edgar

* The author recorded spiritual messages from Kuni-no-Tokotachi-no-Kami, an ancient Japanese god, immediately before this session.

Cayce usually coordinates the spirit to call on specific occasions.

Since *Kuni-no-Tokotachi-no-Kami* managed to push aside Edgar Cayce to talk to me, I am not sure what is going on between them.

Well then, Edgar Cayce, Edgar Cayce's spirit. Please come down to Happy Science and reveal to us your thoughts on the sufferings and hardships of Japan and the world now.

[*About five seconds of silence.*]

Comments on "Spiritual Messages from Kuni-no-Tokotachi-no-Kami"

EDGAR CAYCE

Huff [*exhales*]. This is Cayce. Hmm.

TAKEDA

Thank you for coming down. To start, I believe you have overheard our session with Kuni-no-

Tokotachi-no-Kami just now. Would you share your opinion on what you heard?

CAYCE

Hmm... [*About five seconds of silence.*] Hmm... I guess he is a god from the Jomon period*. I'd think he's a god from around that time. He might be a god from the time when people were working hard to make the country of *Wa* (an ancient Japanese country) independent somehow.

But at the foundation, they had received many things from China, even though they may have had an independent spirit. He might not know much about the United States since it's a recently established country.

TAKEDA

It seems like he wants to protect his own country from China by isolating it.

* A Japanese prehistoric period, from about 12,000 to 2,400 years ago.

CAYCE
After all, the origins of the country lie in the ambushing of Chinese coastal regions to steal treasures and those forces gaining the power to start dynasties.

Modern medicine is losing against the novel coronavirus

TAKEDA
According to Kuni-no-Tokotachi-no-Kami, the novel coronavirus pandemic will kill about five million people in Japan, a country that makes up about 1 percent of the world population. What do you think of this estimate?

CAYCE
Now, there are 100 people, right?

TAKEDA
About 100 deaths.

CAYCE

So, it's a gamble right now. They expect the infections to slow down if they tell people to stay home for a month and reduce human contact by 80 percent. Without medicine to counter the virus in the current conditions, they are simply guessing that the influenza medicine might be slightly effective.

In reality, they are taking a very primitive approach. They are telling people that the virus will not spread as long as people don't meet each other, which means the activities of civilization will stop. So, it is not clear whether "one month" means the amount of time to stop the activities or the amount of time humans can endure. It is a fine line.

Right now, the news reports suggest that the spread has stopped in China. If this is true, it might be possible to stop the infection from spreading further. But if not, meaning if a second or third wave of infections were to occur in China, this pandemic would be less likely to stop.

The fact that it's spreading worldwide shows how serious this is. Like in the United States... This time, developed countries like the United States, Spain, Italy, Germany, the U.K., and France have suffered considerable damage. It almost seems like the countries with advanced medicine are suffering more casualties. This means people are trying to fight using medicine, but are losing.

There are other countries with casualties as well, but it's difficult to grasp the true number. They probably don't know because they don't have medical institutions. So, the actual number should be far greater than what is reported. Right now, it is said that more than one million people in the world are infected, but there is no doubt that the actual number is much higher.

Eventually, the infection will spread to the point where the total number of cases will double in two days. It could escalate that far since there aren't any clear countermeasures now. If the virus weren't spreading in the United States and were only spreading within some other country, I believe the U.S. president would've been driven to impulsively set that country on fire. But since it's spreading worldwide, nothing could be done to solve the situation.

How far will the infection spread?

CAYCE
Once it ultimately spreads to about half, there will be many individuals who develop antibodies to the virus, so the spread should stop around that time.

TAKEDA
Are you saying the infection will spread that far?

CAYCE
It's possible.

TAKEDA
Are you saying the chances are high?

CAYCE
Yes.

JINMU
When you say "half," do you mean that half of the world population will be infected?

CAYCE
That's right. That's about four billion people. It's possible.

JINMU
So, you're saying that's how far the infection could spread.

CAYCE
Yes.

TAKEDA
About how many people would you expect to die in that case?

CAYCE
People can't stand this. Even if they are told to stay put at home without meeting other people, realistically, this is impossible. Improved transportation and better means to travel are the characteristics of the current civilization. That is what the current civilization is about. (Staying put) would be like living in a hole in the ground and denying the current civilization.

I don't think people will be able to tolerate that for much longer. Take countries that are close to each other, for example. If one country is less strict and an explosive increase in infection occurs there, the infection is bound to spread to the neighboring countries, at which point it couldn't be stopped. It would be difficult to stop the spread, especially since the world is now interconnected through trade. I don't think this will end in one month.

ISONO
How long do you expect this to continue?

CAYCE
Hmm, I expect it to continue for two years before we see any decline.

ISONO
At least two years?

CAYCE
After two years, we will slowly see various countermeasures taking shape. Japan is getting ready to use the current influenza medicine, but using it excessively comes with a side effect: an

increase in birth defects. So, I think it will be prohibited in a year.

The coronavirus death toll in the worst-case scenario

ISONO

At the moment, the pandemic is spreading all over the world, and countries are now being given the task of figuring out a way to stop it. In response, they are practicing social distancing, or in other words, creating more space between people in social settings, not leaving the house, and isolating themselves in hopes of preventing the infection from spreading further. Is this actually effective? Or, is there another, more effective way to stop or slow down the rate of infection?

CAYCE

Hmm. In reality, it's impossible to stop the spreading at this stage. The coronavirus entering humans is causing them to become like viruses which should be avoided, so the only way to counter that will be to sanitize the entire city by scattering disinfectants from above via a helicopter. But if this is done, people won't be able to live. So, a countermeasure...

The people who survive the viral infection will have antibodies, but it will take about two to three years to create a vaccine from them. Once enough people have this antibody, "resistance" will begin. But right now, the virus is still spreading, so we cannot confirm this just yet.

So, in the worst-case scenario, the infection could spread to half of the population. Once half of the population becomes infected and if the death rate can be minimized to 20 percent at most, then 80 percent of them will have the antibody. I believe the virus will begin to perish from that point. If you were to ask me how many people would die, based on my calculations, the death toll could go up to about 800 million.

Japan could become like how it was at the end of WWII

ISONO

To what extent will Japan…

CAYCE

Hmm. It depends on how Japan handles it. Japan is an island nation, so if people from other countries bring in the virus, it will spread again. If you are asking how long Japan will last as a nation, there is a high chance Japan won't last more than one or two years, much like in World War II. Japan might survive if the infection begins to decline before then, but instead, Japan might fall before the infection starts to settle around the rest of the world. If it cannot survive independently, it will have to keep importing from other countries, so infection is inevitable.

Right now, Japan cannot survive with domestic resources alone. However, I doubt

Japanese people are thinking about this. They probably expect things to return to how they were in the next month or two, so the government will be extremely slow. They are distributing masks and conducting various clinical trials of drugs, but these things easily take two to three years to complete. If the infection increases explosively in a neighboring country, I'm not sure how things will turn out.

Right now, the virus is spreading considerably in the oil-producing regions as well as in the friendly nations of Australia and the United States. In the case where interactions with these countries through airplanes and ships are blocked, Japan could become like how it was at the end of WWII.

One simulation of "the last day on Earth" is about to happen

TAKEDA

Right now, the Japanese government has declared a state of emergency, and as you just mentioned, they are telling people to avoid going outdoors and requesting them to take time off from work to decrease the interaction between people. As compensation, the government is planning to distribute cash. If this continues, economic activities will stagnate and we will face an economic crisis. In your opinion, what will happen to the Japanese economy from here on out?

CAYCE

The developed countries will be hit harder by this disease. As the primary sector of economy ends, the secondary sector... The primary sector is agriculture and fishery, the secondary sector is manufacturing, the tertiary sector is services, and the quaternary sector is computing and other high-tech software industries. So, the more developed a country is, the higher they are on this list. They live their lives without both feet on the ground. This means they don't have their own agriculture and manufacturing, which is quite a significant factor. So, the pandemic has much power to destroy developed countries. It is a very tough situation for them if their people are not allowed to meet, gather in one place, or work in groups.

There are various simulations of the last day on Earth, such as volcanic eruptions, rising sea levels, great earthquakes, tsunami, devastation, and viral outbreak all over the world, or alien attacks, and one of them is about to happen. It has been prophesied over and over again that a pandemic might occur and that such pandemics are more likely to happen when the population increases explosively. The biggest problem concerns China. They have lifted the lockdown in Wuhan, making it appear as though the infection has settled. The biggest issue is whether this is true or not.

Another lesson is that there will be a need to reconsider the military industry. Not only have many people faced hardship from radioactive contamination due to nuclear weapons, but they have also suffered from chemical weapons. The world, however, has not fully experienced contamination through biological weaponry yet. The damage will be tremendous because there will be a chain reaction. It won't just be the pandemic; other things like regional conflicts, war, plunder economy, or invasions could occur due to the chain reaction. Moreover, people will be driven to madness, so many things will occur, including more abnormal crimes and murder. I believe so.

The pandemic is spreading in developed nations where religion is prevalent. In those areas, things are moving in the opposite direction. There could also come a time when people are treated like "animals with a pathogen." If this happens, something like Nazism could reappear. People could be isolated. It will be extremely difficult for you to keep stating what is right while maintaining a healthy mind.

In Japan's case, factors to make food, raw materials, machines, or houses may still be needed, but the people in more sophisticated industries like the service sector will suffer considerable damage. In reality, there will be a great impact on the travel industry, hotel industry, department stores, and distribution industry. The demand for some videos on online streaming media is increasing, but it might not last long. Since people are told to stay home, there has been some demand for games, but that won't last forever.

So, this is a terrifying test. It might feel as if one of the seals from the Book of Revelation was opened.

2

Are There Any Effective Countermeasures to the Coronavirus Pandemic?

Countries need to become more self-sufficient

TAKEDA
What is the most effective economic countermeasure we can take immediately?

CAYCE
Since people cannot go out, distributing money won't lead to consumption. Maybe they will eventually have goods dropped from the sky. It may be similar to how goods are dropped over a refugee camp. Deliveries on land could be stopped because they can spread infection.

If you were to ask me whether infection can be avoided, I believe it's quite difficult because all living things that breathe oxygen are in danger. Now, we are finding out that animals can also be infected. This includes pets, zoo animals, wild animals, and livestock that become our food. If they can get infected, this means the meat industry will also be contaminated by this virus. Considering tigers can be infected, it may not be so difficult for cows, pigs, and chickens to be infected.

TAKEDA
Then, are you suggesting there is a need to increase self-sufficiency?

CAYCE
Yes, there is. Of course, it's necessary. You must not expect help from other countries. The whole world is contaminated at the same time and each country is sending an SOS signal. If a superpower were safe, they could save others, but the whole world is contaminated at this same moment, so it means this was the weakness of an advanced, modern society.

Some kind of mass contamination was bound to happen, especially since many things, such as nuclear missiles, were being developed. If this pandemic had not occurred, a nuclear war could have occurred instead. There are other possibilities.

The United States might wage war on China

TAKEDA
Some people are saying that the virus leaked from a Chinese institution where biological weapons were being developed.

CAYCE
Ah, the United States is already researching that. Right now, the United States in particular is independently looking into that without trusting the WHO (World Health Organization). Once they conclude that as the cause, they are highly likely to wage war.

TAKEDA
I believe there is a clear difference between leaking the virus by accident and doing it intentionally. If China leaked the virus on purpose, they might be carrying out their plan to rule the world after having developed a vaccine. What do you think China will do next?

CAYCE
If they spread the virus abroad after having made the viral weapon in the first place, testing it, leaking it, sacrificing the people of Wuhan while developing a vaccine, and further testing how effective the vaccine is, then hmm... I'm sure the U.S. president is ready to declare war on China. I think he will.

If China's claim of not having any new cases of infections and deaths is true, it would mean that they were also researching some kind of preventative measure at the same time and that they were testing how well it works against the infection after spreading the virus. But if they were lying about their numbers and the infection is actually spreading, they would be in the same state as the other countries. Anyhow, there must be something more if the infection is spreading more in the United States, Spain, and Italy than it is in China.

TAKEDA
Right.

CAYCE
This is hard to believe, considering China's landmass and population.

TAKEDA
Another spirit said that there might be a different virus spreading in those countries.*

* The interviewer is referring to the spirit of Shibasaburo Kitasato (1853-1931), a Japanese bacteriologist. The author recorded "Spiritual Messages from Shibasaburo Kitasato" on March 30, 2020. It is scheduled to be translated and published in July 2020.

CAYCE
Uh-huh. So, I think the U.S. is researching the cause and the countermeasure at the same time. The world's greatest city, New York, is driven to the point where not a single soul can be seen. This is just one of many nightmares they've repeatedly illustrated in movies. It's one of their stories. They have many such simulations and have various countermeasures against them. They know how to respond to each situation. So, they are researching this now.

The only thing that can calm this crisis is the Advent of the Great Savior

CAYCE
In any case, you have a humanitarian crisis. As of today (April 9, 2020), the infection has spread to over 1.4 million confirmed cases. This is the number of confirmed individuals. There are many more who have not been tested at hospitals.

Over 1.4 million confirmed to be infected. This means there should be about 10 million people actually infected, so this number should continue to rise with time. Generally, people don't bother to go to a hospital to be tested, so there should be more infected people under the surface.

Moreover, we don't know who has the antibodies, but the people who are meant to survive will survive. There is no question about that. The people who are meant to survive will survive, and there will be those who won't. This kind of "sorting" will begin. The survivors will be treated differently depending on whether they survived because they were not infected or because they had immunity.

In any case, I view this hardship... I think the Olympics next year will most likely be canceled. That is an understatement, seeing as the infection is spreading all over the world. Even if Japan manages to keep the number of cases small or even makes it appear as such, the Olympics can't be held. Usually, not being able to hold the Olympics means a war is coming. I guess humanity has become too dangerous after having developed too many weapons.

So, in a way, there might be a self-cleansing power at work, applying pressure to reduce the human population. I've heard there are over 10,000 cases of the "corona scam" in Japan. Such crimes are becoming rampant in Japan, so I believe things could be even worse in other countries. There will be many cases of murder and other crimes, such as burglary and theft, and ultimately, people who have gone mad might bring machine guns and shoot infected people.

To calm this situation... Japan might be the last to accept this, but from a global perspective, the Advent of the Great Savior is the only answer. Many countries will hope for the Advent of a Savior. This will be the majority.

Now is the time to have faith in El Cantare

CAYCE
El Cantare was reborn for the first time in 150 million years, so a significant crisis was bound to occur. The crisis of humankind will come. But it won't go as far as (the flood narrative of) "Noah's Ark." Just one family survived in that case, so it's very unlikely for the same thing to happen.

A new faith will appear. People will ask to be saved. They will seek salvation, and if the preexisting religions can't save them, a new form of salvation must come down. After all, people who believe in God make up over two-thirds of the world.

So, unlike the ideas of Kuni-no-Tokotachi-no-Kami, I believe faith in El Cantare will spread suddenly and globally, like a pandemic. As for Japan, I don't know what would happen; it might spread before or after that. This faith will mainly gain popularity in a particular country or several countries.

What you are saying is correct. This pandemic will settle down through faith and devotion to the true God, and your missionary work. The power of El Cantare is… I'm sure the materialistic weekly tabloids will make a fuss if I say this, but the power of El Cantare is superior to the propagating power of the coronavirus. It's clearly stronger. We need a light that covers the entire Earth to suppress this outbreak. We cannot expel the coronavirus which has spread all over the world unless there is such light.

I am not suggesting fishing in troubled waters. I believe people must call the name of God. Now is the time for faith. Some people might talk about the disease spreading in gatherings of misguided beliefs or powerless religious groups, but that's a judgment made based on a value-neutral stance. You could wait a month to see how things turn out, but after some time, you must be positive and start your missionary work. Now is the time to listen to the voice of the true God.

3
The Power to Expel the Coronavirus

The coronavirus can be defeated with God's Light

CAYCE
The following are the most effective tools to repel the coronavirus: Ryuho Okawa's lectures, books, DVDs, CDs, movies, music, and all things sent out from Happy Science. They are all effective.

Of course, Happy Science is quite big, so there will be followers who end up getting infected, but there should also be many people who recover from infections.

Viruses are small, but they come in great numbers. When a few of them enter your body through droplet transmission and stay there, they will find their way into your lungs and then into your bloodstream, working to contaminate your whole body. This is a form of possession. It is almost the same as a "zombie-style" mass possession.

Viruses mass possess people. This is the same as spiritual possession, so it is possible to drive out whatever that is possessing you. Ten years ago, I spoke about how the Legion* would come and make you suffer a lot, and also how Pandora's box would be opened. The Legion will come.

There will be other terrible things to come... "scorching hell," "freezing hell,"† and natural disasters. There are many other things written. El Cantare will save you from all these.

For the time being, you might be hiding quietly according to the government's request, but even if the old religions die out, faith in the

* The name of a demon or group of demons depicted in the New Testament. In "Future Readings by Edgar Cayce" recorded on June 1, 2010, Cayce said, "There will break out a malignant disease humanity has never seen. The Legion has already been released."

† Here, "scorching hell" and "freezing hell" mean global heating and global cooling, respectively. In the aforementioned "Future Readings by Edgar Cayce," Cayce also said, "After global heating, there might come volcanic eruptions, then global cooling. After scorching hell, there will come freezing hell."

new God will cover the Earth and destroy the coronavirus. This is a battle. You (Happy Science) are the new religion born for that. Kuni-no-Tokotachi-no-Kami spoke as if the 30 some years proved to be useless, but you can also say that it took 30 some years to create the foundation. The footing has been established both in Japan and the world, so you should be fully prepared to spread this teaching.

It (novel coronavirus) behaves similarly to the viruses that cause colds and the flu. It enters deep into your body, goes in and out of your lungs, infects your cells, and eventually turns your live cells into dead ones. This is something you can defeat with God's Light. Many materialists and atheists might die, but there will be new faith—people who believe in the true God will be saved and the millennial kingdom will be established.

It (viral infection) is really a form of possession. It's easy to tell possession by a human spirit, but this is possession by something much smaller. Viruses possess you in cloud-like groups, boost their energy, and multiply themselves. They are now trying to spread across the world in this way.

So, the question is, "What can eradicate all of this?" The only answer is, "Faith in God." It means there is the teaching that can save people on a global scale. Japan is unable to believe this from their common sense nowadays, so they are saying things like medicine is collapsing and only thinking of ways to build more hospitals or to get more medical workers. Unfortunately, those things won't be effective. Isolation is the only way. Even the people caring for the patients end up getting infected.

Frankly, for those who are staying home, you should read books, listen to lectures, or listen to music (from Happy Science)... Plus, the movie theaters where the Happy Science movie will be played shouldn't be closed. It would be better for people to go there rather than to stay home. Something much stronger than droplet transmission is emitted from there.

Many serious diseases and rare illnesses were cured when people watched last year's movie, *Immortal Hero* (Executive Producer Ryuho Okawa, released in 2019), so there is no question your movies carry enough power to defeat the coronavirus. You should be making more films, and not holding back. Now is the time when harmful, hellish things should be rejected and good things should be spread. It's also a time of choice.

Give back to God what is God's

CAYCE
Hospitals are helpful from a physical perspective, but many of them are under the "materialistic umbrella." They must give back to God what is God's. I guess, depending on who they refer to

as "God," my opinion will differ from the spirit earlier (Kuni-no-Tokotachi-no-Kami).

I believe now is the time when Happy Science must spread around the world. There may be people who ridicule the Happiness Realization Party by saying they haven't been able to win even after 11 years, but I'd like to say to them, "You will experience great suffering because of your ridicule. Turn over a new leaf and listen earnestly to the voice of God. Of course, misfortune will fall on those who ignore the voice of God when it is readily available. Be honest and listen." You must not let hellish novels sell well while God's words go unread. A battle will occur.

In a world where materialistic medicine and treatment spread, people who spread the Truth might appear to be insane, but I think it's the mission of the apostles of the Truth to push back such opinions and carry out the activities to save the people. In any case, your life in this world is limited. There is a power working to push the life span of nearly 100 years back to 50 years again. For people who don't think they have much time left in their lives or who believe that their biological life is short, please engage in your missionary work thinking that this is your last service (to the Lord), as there would be nothing wrong with dying from a mere pneumonia infection.

If you leave the current situation as it is, those who are over 80 years old will be treated like bulk trash as if being tossed in the *ubasuteyama**... This will happen if there is an excess national debt. So, now is the time for those people to do missionary work.

A plague spread in Japan during Emperor Shomu and Empress Komyo's time, but they built the Great Buddha statue at that time (752 AD). They built the Great Buddha of Nara knowing that faith must be strengthened at such times. They spent double the amount of the national

* A mountain in Japanese folklore where old people were abandoned.

budget to build the Great Buddha statue, but the people of Japan were more than willing to offer money for it. So, by nature, Japanese people believe that true faith will modernize and rebuild the country. If I were to share similar opinions as the earlier spirit's, now is the time to emphasize such virtues of Japan.

Happy Science must be more active. There will be headwind and criticism for some time, but the foundation is already complete. It's high time the organizations that support such activities appeared. People are stuck at home not being able to do anything anyway, so you should be asking them if they'd like to help you with activities of the Truth. Such a time has come.

I don't think Happy Science will perish after being oppressed, like how the Oomoto religion did, because your scale and level of teachings are quite different. I know you are different because people of other countries can understand the content of Happy Science teachings. So, please continue with your activities believing that "faith immunity" will win against the coronavirus.

You cannot maintain your life in this world forever, but the soul you have as a human is an eternal one. You will be judged solely on how you lived your life in this world (after you die), so how unselfishly you live your life is what's important.

Fight the battle to stop the coronavirus and truly save the people

CAYCE

If people continue to seclude themselves, avoid contact with people out of fear and only think about staying still, this world will turn into a subterranean hell, where people are secluded underground. So, at some point, you should stop the mass media from stirring up fear like an inflating bubble, and you must change your organization into one that quietly does what needs to be done. Right now, you should be telling people of the Advent of the Great Savior from different angles. Now is the time to save people.

There is a chance the government will prohibit gatherings and impose fines among other things. In the U.K., people are already being penalized for gathering in groups of three or more people in public. This makes it close to impossible for religions to conduct their activities. I guess the governments won't say much as long as everyone does their activities in their own home, so Happy Science needs to be more active through their "sleeping" missionary houses and other locations.

Almost all "clouds of coronavirus" of the normal level can be expelled by listening to Ryuho Okawa's lectures for an hour. It is also important to continue to polish your mind and to use this as an opportunity to spread the idea clearly telling right from wrong, good from evil. This is a battle. If you keep going as it is, the number of infected cases and deaths could reach 4 billion and 800 million, respectively. That's why I'm saying this is a battle. It's a battle to bring a stop to this. When people find out that a power to stop this infection is working in a specific region, they will follow it.

If it weren't for such a situation, the teachings wouldn't spread to these so-called developed countries. The traditional (religious) teachings can't save them. This is clear seeing how far the infection has spread in Italy. The prayers of the Vatican aren't being heard. However, the prayers of Happy Science surely reach the highest level of heaven. You need to create this kind of world.

4

What We Should Keep in Mind When Doing Our Missionary Work under Outing Regulations

CAYCE

Ah, I've spoken too much on my own. If you have any questions, I'll answer them.

ISONO

Thank you very much for teaching us many things. We have strengthened our resolve and we firmly believe that now is indeed the time to spread the light under our faith in the Lord.

We would like to ask you another question. We strongly believe that now is the time for us to really spread the faith and teachings of the Lord, but on the other hand, the government requested we stay home, refrain from engaging in activities, and not go outside. Furthermore, the media outlets are also spreading this view, so we are in an unfavorable environment to conduct our activities. How should we spread the light against headwind from the government or the mass media? We would greatly appreciate it if you could provide us with the words to persuade them or the thoughts to counter such headwinds.

Each person must be proactive in their missionary work and spread the name, "El Cantare"

CAYCE

They are saying to stay home, so it's the perfect time to study the Truth by reading books or listening to lectures. That would be a good idea.

Things depend on how you think about them. So far, you have depended too heavily on Master Okawa's large-scale events to spread the teachings, but instead, you should... If they are prohibiting gatherings of three or more, then all you have to do is to get together in pairs. You can spread the teachings on a one-on-one basis. So, each person must be proactive in their missionary work.

There were many miracles of illnesses being cured last year (2019). We plan to make miracles happen this time, too. We plan to make miracles of defeating the coronavirus, so you will hear more about them in different places*. Anyone is free to decide whether this is non-scientific, but it is a battle to see which side people will believe.

Whether you can engage in activities publicly will depend on your comprehensive judgment, but it is the mission of religion to save people in times of plague, famine, war, earthquakes, typhoons, tsunamis, volcanic eruptions, and all such events. So, people need true guidance in such times. In the end, a one-phrase teaching is

---

* Happy Science has received reports of people recovering from serious cases of the novel coronavirus infection in London, New York, and many other places. They recovered after taking the ritual prayer, "Prayer for Defeating the Novel Coronavirus Infection Originated in China" (available at all Happy Science temples and branches around the world).

enough. Ultimately, there was a single teaching to save people (in the olden days of Japan), such as only chanting "Namu Amida Butsu" (Devotion to Amitabha Buddha) or "Namu Myoho Renge Kyo" (Devotion to the Wonderful Teachings of the Lotus Sutra). So, it is enough to tell them that God, named "El Cantare," has come down to this world. That will replace "Namu Amida Butsu" and "Namu Myoho Renge Kyo." Upholding and spreading the name El Cantare alone counts as missionary work.

So, the spirit earlier who calls himself a god said, "I don't know El Cantare," but if so, he must learn the name. You must spread the slogans, "Let's pray to El Cantare," "Let's learn about El Cantare," and "Let's study the teachings of El Cantare" to the world through various means... There are more than enough ways to disseminate information now. Right?

Notify people of such information instead of informing them of the death toll. Just tell them,

"El Cantare shall save you." "Amitabha Buddha shall save you" spread far and wide (in Japan) a long time ago, when there were fewer methods of communication, so this is a similar opportunity.

But this doesn't mean you should do everything that goes against laws and regulations. There are many other things you could do that don't go against the laws and regulations. It just means you should do those things instead. That's what I think.

If someone doesn't know El Cantare because He is a foreign god like the "god made in Japan" said earlier, Happy Science members should start a surging movement to invite such people to get to know El Cantare more. It's getting more difficult for people to vote in these conditions, so you shouldn't only think about using worldly means.

I believe Happy Science has a good level of trust in society. Some weekly magazines ridicule Happy Science, but they can write such things because you are as credible and powerful as the government and ruling party. Other religions aren't even worth criticizing because they don't have any power, but Happy Science has a powerful ability to spread information.

So now, you should be more concise and say, "Believe in the name of El Cantare and recite it. Pray to El Cantare." It is enough to tell them, "First, pray to El Cantare." This is free. Tell them to pray, OK? You're not doing this for profit. Just tell them the words, "Pray to El Cantare." That's enough. If they want to learn more about El Cantare, they have many ways they can do so, of course.

Since you're in such a tough situation now, you must work hard to continue to build more branches in Japan and overseas starting next year, as long as construction companies are working. Because the pandemic is happening, now is the time for you to build more branches.

Happy Science teachings are about to spread widely across the world

TAKEDA
Thank you very much for giving us your valuable messages today. We, members of Happy Science, will work to become more active in our missionary activities around the world and spread the Lord's light to every corner of the world to defeat this virus.

CAYCE
We are also about to explode. An "overshoot" (an explosive increase). What we have been holding in for over 30 years is about to "overshoot" and spread widely all over the world. It's the same. This is a battle to destroy the pandemic.

TAKEDA
We will carry out our activities ardently, so that heaven will shine its light on us.

CAYCE

(Other religions can't cure illnesses) Because the light won't come down, right? It won't shine on the Christian churches, Shinto shrines, or Buddhist temples, right? But there is a place where it is coming down.

You could go to the Vatican, but Jesus is not hearing the pope's prayers. The pope is not being answered by Jesus. But here, Jesus is listening. You are receiving answers. Jesus is working as a disciple (of El Cantare). Such a place exists, so why won't people pray? Why won't they believe?

You don't need to be concerned with small matters like the government or the prime minister who will be resigning soon. You should do more of what needs to be done as the main work of religion.

TAKEDA

Yes, OK. We will do our best.

CAYCE
OK.

TAKEDA
Thank you.

5

After the Recording

RYUHO OKAWA

[*Claps once.*] That was Cayce.

As expected, Edgar Cayce seems to have a broader perspective. According to our judgment, he is one of the Seven Archangels, Sariel, and in the East, he is also said to be ranked as Bhaisajyaguru (a tathagata of medicine). If he has a connection to Bhaisajyaguru, he is in a position to fight this kind of disease. In truth, many of his 14,000 readings done when he was alive were medical, so I think he is knowledgeable about such matters.

Now, people are only thinking from a materialistic perspective. They only talk about masks and flu medicine and only think about constructing buildings to put sick people in. They are only thinking about locking up people in hotels*, which is no different from putting infected people in that luxury cruise ship†. The infection rate is probably the highest in hospitals. I think that's true. You shouldn't go there.

TAKEDA
No, we shouldn't.

RYUHO OKAWA
People who aren't in critical condition shouldn't go. Also, the virus seems to be spreading more in places where people traditionally bury bodies instead of cremating them, so it might be a better idea to cremate the bodies of people who died from the viral infection. Places that lack crematoriums might see more problems.

*At the time of the recording, Japan was implementing a policy where the local governments rent hotels to accommodate patients with mild cases of the novel coronavirus infection.

† The cruise ship Diamond Princess, with approximately 3,700 people on board, was quarantined for two weeks in Yokohama port starting February 3, 2020, after some of the passengers who disembarked in Hong Kong were found to be infected by the novel coronavirus. But a cluster infection broke out on the ship, infecting over 700 people.

This is a battle. I guess we, Happy Science, will have to strengthen ourselves for battle as much as we can.

TAKEDA
We will fight.

RYUHO OKAWA
OK.

TAKEDA
Thank you.

RYUHO OKAWA
[*Claps twice.*] OK. Yes.

Afterword

Around the time when *Spiritual Reading of Novel Coronavirus Infection Originated in China* was published in February, I remember the number of infected people was a little over 40,000, and the death toll was less than 1,000 people worldwide.

I assume the Japanese government was ready to invite Chinese President Xi Jinping as a state guest around the time the cherry blossoms bloomed, and carry out the Tokyo Olympics and Paralympics in the summer of 2020.

Now it is the middle of April, and the number of infected people has reached two million while the death toll has passed 100,000 around the world. The Japanese government and the leaders of the major powers are doing everything they can to make the pandemic end in another month or so, but they have not thought about what might happen if the pandemic continues thereafter.

All they are doing is encouraging everyone to "stay home" and screaming out about the "collapse of the healthcare system." This book poses a fundamental question about their predictions of the future. And it teaches the importance of "faith immunity." The good shall listen to this voice.

Ryuho Okawa
Master & CEO of Happy Science Group
April 15, 2020

ABOUT THE AUTHOR

RYUHO OKAWA was born on July 7th 1956, in Tokushima, Japan. After graduating from the University of Tokyo with a law degree, he joined a Tokyo-based trading house. While working at its New York headquarters, he studied international finance at the Graduate Center of the City University of New York. In 1981, he attained Great Enlightenment and became aware that he is El Cantare with a mission to bring salvation to all of humankind. In 1986 he established Happy Science. It now has members in over 100 countries across the world, with more than 700 local branches and temples as well as 10,000 missionary houses around the world. The total number of lectures has exceeded 3,100 (of which more than 150 are in English) and over 2,650 books (of which more than 550 are Spiritual Interview Series) have been published, many of which are translated into 31 languages. Many of the books, including *The Laws of the Sun* have become best sellers or million sellers. To date, Happy Science has produced 20 movies. The original story and original concept were given by the Executive Producer Ryuho Okawa. Recent movie titles are *The Real Exorcist* (live-action, May 2020), *Kiseki to no Deai - Kokoro ni Yorisou 3 -* (lit. "Encounters with Miracles - Heart to Heart 3 -," documentary scheduled to be released in Aug. 2020), and *Twiceborn* (live-action, Fall of 2020). He has also composed the lyrics and music of over 100 songs, such as theme songs and featured songs of movies. Moreover, he is the Founder of Happy Science University and Happy Science Academy (Junior and Senior High School), Founder and President of the Happiness Realization Party, Founder and Honorary Headmaster of Happy Science Institute of Government and Management, Founder of IRH Press Co., Ltd., and the Chairperson of New Star Production Co., Ltd. and ARI Production Co., Ltd.

WHAT IS EL CANTARE?

El Cantare means "the Light of the Earth," and is the Supreme God of the Earth who has been guiding humankind since the beginning of Genesis. He is whom Jesus called Father and Muhammad called Allah. Different parts of El Cantare's core consciousness have descended to Earth in the past, once as Alpha and another as Elohim. His branch spirits, such as Shakyamuni Buddha and Hermes, have descended to Earth many times and helped to flourish many civilizations. To unite various religions and to integrate various fields of study in order to build a new civilization on Earth, a part of the core consciousness has descended to Earth as Master Ryuho Okawa.

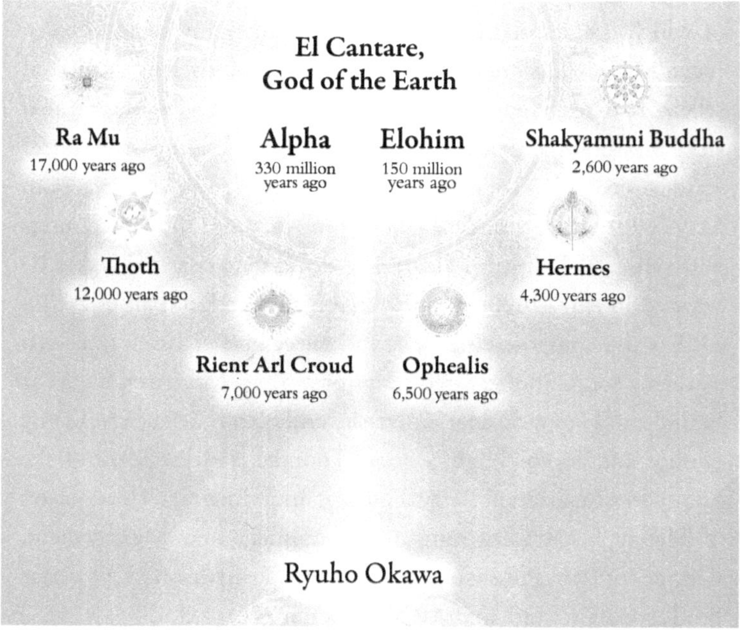

Alpha is a part of the core consciousness of El Cantare who descended to Earth around 330 million years ago. Alpha preached Earth's Truths to harmonize and unify Earth-born humans and space people who came from other planets.

Elohim is a part of El Cantare's core consciousness who descended to Earth around 150 million years ago. He gave wisdom, mainly on the differences of light and darkness, good and evil.

Shakyamuni Buddha was born as a prince into the Shakya Clan in India around 2,600 years ago. When he was 29 years old, he renounced the world and sought enlightenment. He later attained Great Enlightenment and founded Buddhism.

Hermes is one of the 12 Olympian gods in Greek mythology, but the spiritual Truth is that he taught the teachings of love and progress around 4,300 years ago that became the origin of the current Western civilization. He is a hero that truly existed.

Ophealis was born in Greece around 6,500 years ago and was the leader who took an expedition to as far as Egypt. He is the God of miracles, prosperity, and arts, and is known as Osiris in the Egyptian mythology.

Rient Arl Croud was born as a king of the ancient Incan Empire around 7,000 years ago and taught about the mysteries of the mind. In the heavenly world, he is responsible for the interactions that take place between various planets.

Thoth was an almighty leader who built the golden age of the Atlantic civilization around 12,000 years ago. In the Egyptian mythology, he is known as god Thoth.

Ra Mu was a leader who built the golden age of the civilization of Mu around 17,000 years ago. As a religious leader and a politician, he ruled by uniting religion and politics.

WHAT IS A SPIRITUAL MESSAGE?

We are all spiritual beings living on this earth. The following is the mechanism behind Master Ryuho Okawa's spiritual messages.

1 You are a spirit

People are born into this world to gain wisdom through various experiences and return to the other world when their lives end. We are all spirits and repeat this cycle in order to refine our souls.

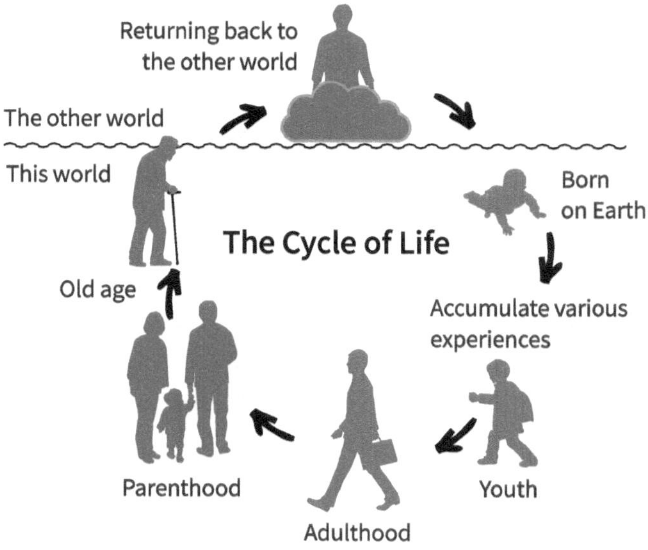

2 You have a guardian spirit

Guardian spirits are those who protect the people who are living on this earth. Each of us has a guardian spirit that watches over us and guides us from the other world. They were us in our past life, and are identical in how we think.

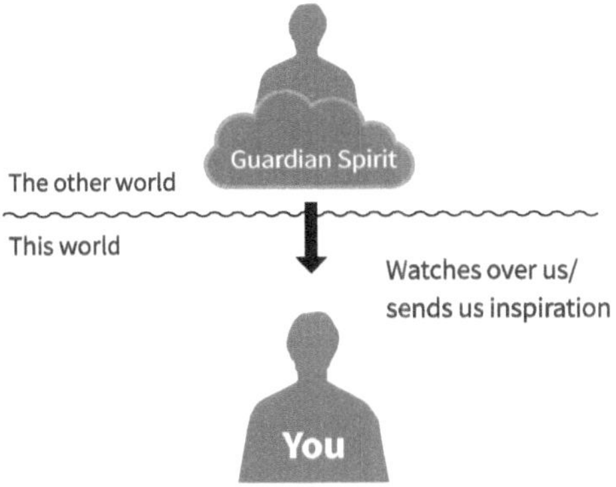

3 How spiritual messages work

Master Ryuho Okawa, through his enlightenment, is capable of summoning any spirit from anywhere in the world, including the spirit world.

Master Okawa's way of receiving spiritual messages is fundamentally different from that of other psychic mediums who undergo trances and are thereby completely taken over by the spirits they are channeling.

Master Okawa's attainment of a high level of enlightenment enables him to retain full control of his consciousness and body throughout the duration of the spiritual message. To allow the spirits to express their own thoughts and personalities freely, however, Master Okawa usually softens the dominancy of his consciousness. This way, he is able to keep his own philosophies out of the way and ensure that the spiritual messages are pure expressions of the spirits he is channeling.

Since guardian spirits think at the same subconscious level as the person living on earth, Master Okawa can summon the spirit and find out what the person on earth is actually thinking. If the person has already returned to the other world, the spirit can give messages to the people living on earth through Master Okawa.

Since 2009, more than 1,050 sessions of spiritual messages have been openly recorded by Master Okawa, and the majority of these have been published. Spiritual messages from the guardian spirits of people living today such as Donald Trump, Japanese Prime Minister Shinzo Abe and Chinese President Xi Jinping, as well as spiritual messages sent from the spirit world by Jesus Christ, Muhammad, Thomas Edison, Mother Teresa, Steve Jobs and Nelson Mandela are just a tiny pack of spiritual messages that were published so far.

Domestically, in Japan, these spiritual messages are being read by a wide range of politicians and mass media, and the high-level contents of these books are delivering an impact even more on politics, news and public opinion. In recent years, there have been spiritual messages recorded in English, and English translations are being done on the spiritual messages given in Japanese. These have been published overseas, one after another, and have started to shake the world.

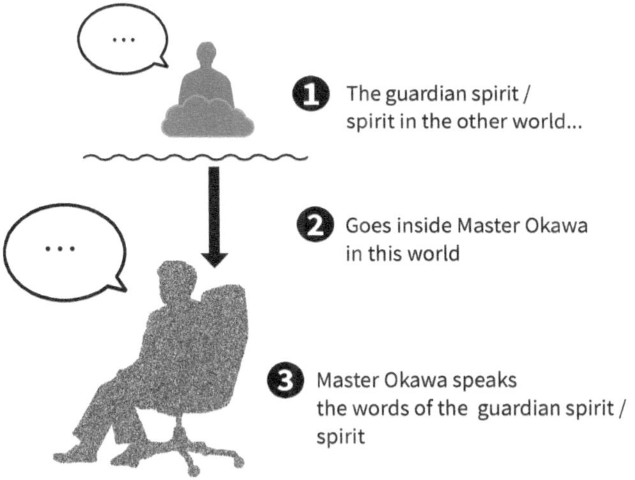

For more about spiritual messages and a complete list of books in the Spiritual Interview Series, visit ***okawabooks.com***

ABOUT HAPPY SCIENCE

Happy Science is a global movement that empowers individuals to find purpose and spiritual happiness and to share that happiness with their families, societies, and the world. With more than twelve million members around the world, Happy Science aims to increase awareness of spiritual truths and expand our capacity for love, compassion, and joy so that together we can create the kind of world we all wish to live in.

Activities at Happy Science are based on the Principles of Happiness (Love, Wisdom, Self-Reflection, and Progress). These principles embrace worldwide philosophies and beliefs, transcending boundaries of culture and religions.

Love teaches us to give ourselves freely without expecting anything in return; it encompasses giving, nurturing, and forgiving.

Wisdom leads us to the insights of spiritual truths, and opens us to the true meaning of life and the will of God (the universe, the highest power, Buddha).

Self-Reflection brings a mindful, nonjudgmental lens to our thoughts and actions to help us find our truest selves—the essence of our souls—and deepen our connection to the highest power. It helps us attain a clean and peaceful mind and leads us to the right life path.

Progress emphasizes the positive, dynamic aspects of our spiritual growth—actions we can take to manifest and spread happiness around the world. It's a path that not only expands our soul growth, but also furthers the collective potential of the world we live in.

PROGRAMS AND EVENTS

The doors of Happy Science are open to all. We offer a variety of programs and events, including self-exploration and self-growth programs, spiritual seminars, meditation and contemplation sessions, study groups, and book events.

Our programs are designed to:

* Deepen your understanding of your purpose and meaning in life
* Improve your relationships and increase your capacity to love unconditionally
* Attain peace of mind, decrease anxiety and stress, and feel positive
* Gain deeper insights and a broader perspective on the world
* Learn how to overcome life's challenges

... and much more.

For more information, visit ***happy-science.org.***

OUR ACTIVITIES

Happy Science does other various activities to provide support for those in need.

- **You Are An Angel! General Incorporated Association**

  Happy Science has a volunteer network in Japan that encourages and supports children with disabilities as well as their parents and guardians.

- **Never Mind School for Truancy**

  At 'Never Mind,' we support students who find it very challenging to attend schools in Japan. We also nurture their self-help spirit and power to rebound against obstacles in life based on Master Okawa's teachings and faith.

- **"Prevention Against Suicide" Campaign since 2003**

  A nationwide campaign to reduce suicides; over 20,000 people commit suicide every year in Japan. "The Suicide Prevention Website-Words of Truth for You-" presents spiritual prescriptions for worries such as depression, lost love, extramarital affairs, bullying and work-related problems, thereby saving many lives.

- **Support for Anti-bullying Campaigns**

  Happy Science provides support for a group of parents and guardians, Network to Protect Children from Bullying, a general incorporated foundation launched in Japan to end bullying, including those that can even be called a criminal offense. So far, the network received more than 5,000 cases and resolved 90% of them.

- **The Golden Age Scholarship**

This scholarship is granted to students who can contribute greatly and bring a hopeful future to the world.

- **Success No.1**
Buddha's Truth Afterschool Academy

Happy Science has over 180 classrooms throughout Japan and in several cities around the world that focus on afterschool education for children. The education focuses on faith and morals in addition to supporting children's school studies.

- **Angel Plan V**

For children under the age of kindergarten, Happy Science holds classes for nurturing healthy, positive, and creative boys and girls.

- **Future Stars Training Department**

The Future Stars Training Department was founded within the Happy Science Media Division with the goal of nurturing talented individuals to become successful in the performing arts and entertainment industry.

- **New Star Production Co., Ltd.**
ARI Production Co., Ltd.

We have companies to nurture actors and actresses, artists, and vocalists. They are also involved in film production.

DOCUMENTARY MOVIE
HEART TO HEART

In this documentary movie, Happy Science University students visit these NPO activities to discover what salvation truly is, and on the meaning of life, through heart-to-heart interviews.

ABOUT HAPPY SCIENCE MOVIES

THE REAL EXORCIST

31 Awards from 6 Countries!

STORY Tokyo —the most mystical city in the world where you find spiritual spots in the most unexpected places. Sayuri works as a part time waitress at a small coffee shop "Extra" where regular customers enjoy the authentic coffee that the owner brews. Meanwhile, Sayuri uses her supernatural powers to help those who are troubled by spiritual phenomena one after another. Through her special consultations, she touches the hearts of the people and helps them by showing the truths of the invisible world.

USA
GOLD REMI AWARD
53rd WorldFest Houston
International Film Festival 2020

MONACO
BEST FEATURE FILM
17th Angel Film Awards
2020
Monaco International Film Festival

NIGERIA
BEST FEATURE FILM
EKO International Film Festival
2020

BEST FEMALE ACTOR
17th Angel Film Awards
2020
Monaco International Film Festival

BEST FEMALE SUPPORTING ACTOR
17th Angel Film Awards
2020
Monaco International Film Festival

BEST SUPPORTING ACTRESS
EKO International Film Festival
2020

BEST VISUAL EFFECTS
17th Angel Film Awards
2020
Monaco International Film Festival

For more information, visit www.realexorcistmovie.com

IMMORTAL HERO
On VOD NOW

Based on the true story of a man whose near death experience inspires him to choose life... and change the lives of millions.

38 Awards from 9 Countries!

SPAIN
BARCELONA INTERNATIONAL FILM FESTIVAL 2019 [THE CASTELL AWARDS]

SPAIN
MADRID INTERNATIONAL FILM FESTIVAL 2019 [BEST DIRECTOR OF A FOREIGN LANGUAGE FEATURE FILM]

ITALY
FLORENCE FILM AWARDS JUL 2019 [HONORABLE MENTION: FEATURE FILM]

USA
INDIE VISIONS FILM FESTIVAL JUL 2019 [WINNER (NARRATIVE FEATURE FILM)]

ITALY
FLORENCE FILM AWARDS JUL 2019 [BEST ORIGINAL SCREENPLAY]

ITALY
DIAMOND FILM AWARDS JUL 2019 [WINNER (NARRATIVE FEATUREFILM)]

...and more!

For more information, visit ***www.immortal-hero.com***

Animation

THE LAWS OF THE UNIVERSE - PART I

Battle requires strength. Harmony requires even more.

7 Awards from 4 Countries!

FRANCE
NICE INTERNATIONAL FILM FESTIVAL 2019
BEST INTERNATIONAL ANIMATION AWARD

UK
LONDON INTERNATIONAL MOTION PICTURE AWARDS 2019
BEST INTERNATIONAL ANIMATION FEATURE FILM AWARD

USA
AWARENESS FILM FESTIVAL [SPECIAL JURY ANIMATION AWARD]

USA
FILM INVASION LOS ANGELES [GRAND JURY PRIZE – BEST ANIME FEATURE]

...and more!

For more information, visit ***https://laws-of-universe.hspicturesstudio.com/***

Documentary

LIFE IS BEAUTIFUL

Six people seeking their purposes of life

BRONZE REMI AWARD
53rd WORLDFEST HOUSTON INTERNATIONAL FILM FESTIVAL 2020

CONTACT INFORMATION

Happy Science is a worldwide organization with faith centers around the globe. For a comprehensive list of centers, visit the worldwide directory at ***happy-science.org***. The following are some of the many Happy Science locations:

UNITED STATES AND CANADA

New York
79 Franklin St., New York, NY 10013
Phone: 212-343-7972
Fax: 212-343-7973
Email: ny@happy-science.org
Website: happyscience-na.org

New Jersey
725 River Rd, #102B, Edgewater, NJ 07020
Phone: 201-313-0127
Fax: 201-313-0120
Email: nj@happy-science.org
Website: happyscience-na.org

Florida
5208 8th St., St. Zephyrhills, FL 33542
Phone: 813-715-0000
Fax: 813-715-0010
Email: florida@happy-science.org
Website: happyscience-na.org

Atlanta
1874 Piedmont Ave., NE Suite 360-C
Atlanta, GA 30324
Phone: 404-892-7770
Email: atlanta@happy-science.org
Website: happyscience-na.org

San Francisco
525 Clinton St.
Redwood City, CA 94062
Phone & Fax: 650-363-2777
Email: sf@happy-science.org
Website: happyscience-na.org

Los Angeles
1590 E. Del Mar Blvd., Pasadena, CA 91106
Phone: 626-395-7775
Fax: 626-395-7776
Email: la@happy-science.org
Website: happyscience-na.org

Orange County
10231 Slater Ave., #204
Fountain Valley, CA 92708
Phone: 714-745-1140
Email: oc@happy-science.org
Website: happyscience-na.org

San Diego
7841 Balboa Ave., Suite #202
San Diego, CA 92111
Phone: 619-381-7615
Fax: 626-395-7776
E-mail: sandiego@happy-science.org
Website: happyscience-na.org

Hawaii
Phone: 808-591-9772
Fax: 808-591-9776
Email: hi@happy-science.org
Website: happyscience-na.org

Kauai
3343 Kanakolu Street, Suite 5
Lihue, HI 96766, U.S.A.
Phone: 808-822-7007
Fax: 808-822-6007
Email: kauai-hi@happy-science.org
Website: kauai.happyscience-na.org

Toronto
845 The Queensway
Etobicoke ON M8Z 1N6 Canada
Phone: 1-416-901-3747
Email: toronto@happy-science.org
Website: happy-science.ca

Vancouver
#201-2607 East 49th Avenue
Vancouver, BC, V5S 1J9, Canada
Phone: 1-604-437-7735
Fax: 1-604-437-7764
Email: vancouver@happy-science.org
Website: happy-science.ca

INTERNATIONAL

Tokyo
1-6-7 Togoshi, Shinagawa
Tokyo, 142-0041 Japan
Phone: 81-3-6384-5770
Fax: 81-3-6384-5776
Email: tokyo@happy-science.org
Website: happy-science.org

Seoul
74, Sadang-ro 27-gil,
Dongjak-gu, Seoul, Korea
Phone: 82-2-3478-8777
Fax: 82-2-3478-9777
Email: korea@happy-science.org
Website: happyscience-korea.org

London
3 Margaret St.
London,W1W 8RE United Kingdom
Phone: 44-20-7323-9255
Fax: 44-20-7323-9344
Email: eu@happy-science.org
Website: happyscience-uk.org

Taipei
No. 89, Lane 155, Dunhua N. Road
Songshan District, Taipei City 105, Taiwan
Phone: 886-2-2719-9377
Fax: 886-2-2719-5570
Email: taiwan@happy-science.org
Website: happyscience-tw.org

Sydney
516 Pacific Hwy, Lane Cove North,
NSW 2066, Australia
Phone: 61-2-9411-2877
Fax: 61-2-9411-2822
Email: sydney@happy-science.org

Malaysia
No 22A, Block 2, Jalil Link Jalan Jalil Jaya 2,
Bukit Jalil 57000, Kuala Lumpur, Malaysia
Phone: 60-3-8998-7877
Fax: 60-3-8998-7977
Email: malaysia@happy-science.org
Website: happyscience.org.my

Brazil Headquarters
Rua. Domingos de Morais 1154,
Vila Mariana, Sao Paulo SP
CEP 04009-002, Brazil
Phone: 55-11-5088-3800
Fax: 55-11-5088-3806
Email: sp@happy-science.org
Website: happyscience.com.br

Nepal
Kathmandu Metropolitan City Ward
No. 15,
Ring Road, Kimdol,
Sitapaila Kathmandu, Nepal
Phone: 97-714-272931
Email: nepal@happy-science.org

Jundiai
Rua Congo, 447, Jd. Bonfiglioli
Jundiai-CEP, 13207-340
Phone: 55-11-4587-5952
Email: jundiai@happy-science.org

Uganda
Plot 877 Rubaga Road, Kampala
P.O. Box 34130, Kampala, Uganda
Phone: 256-79-4682-121
Email: uganda@happy-science.org
Website: happyscience-uganda.org

ABOUT HAPPINESS REALIZATION PARTY

The Happiness Realization Party (HRP) was founded in May 2009 by Master Ryuho Okawa as part of the Happy Science Group to offer concrete and proactive solutions to the current issues such as military threats from North Korea and China and the long-term economic recession. HRP aims to implement drastic reforms of the Japanese government, thereby bringing peace and prosperity to Japan. To accomplish this, HRP proposes two key policies:

1) Strengthening the national security and the Japan-U.S. alliance, which plays a vital role in the stability of Asia.

2) Improving the Japanese economy by implementing drastic tax cuts, taking monetary easing measures and creating new major industries.

HRP advocates that Japan should offer a model of a religious nation that allows diverse values and beliefs to coexist, and that contributes to global peace.

For more information, visit ***en.hr-party.jp***

ABOUT IRH PRESS

IRH Press Co., Ltd., based in Tokyo, was founded in 1987 as a publishing division of Happy Science. IRH Press publishes religious and spiritual books, journals, magazines and also operates broadcast and film production enterprises. For more information, visit *okawabooks.com*.

Follow us on:
Facebook: Okawa Books
Twitter: Okawa Books
Goodreads: Ryuho Okawa
Instagram: OkawaBooks
Pinterest: Okawa Books

RYUHO OKAWA'S LAWS SERIES

The Laws Series is an annual volume of books that are mainly comprised of Ryuho Okawa's lectures on various topics that highlight principles and guidelines for the activities of Happy Science every year. *The Laws of the Sun*, the first publication of the Laws Series, ranked in the annual best-selling list in Japan in 1987. Since then, all of the Laws Series' titles have ranked in the annual best-selling list for more than two decades, setting sociocultural trends in Japan and around the world.

THE TRILOGY

The first three volumes of the Laws Series, *The Laws of the Sun*, *The Golden Laws*, and *The Nine Dimensions* make a trilogy that completes the basic framework of the teachings of God's Truths. *The Laws of the Sun* discusses the structure of God's Laws, *The Golden Laws* expounds on the doctrine of time, and *The Nine Dimensions* reveals the nature of space.

BOOKS BY RYUHO OKAWA

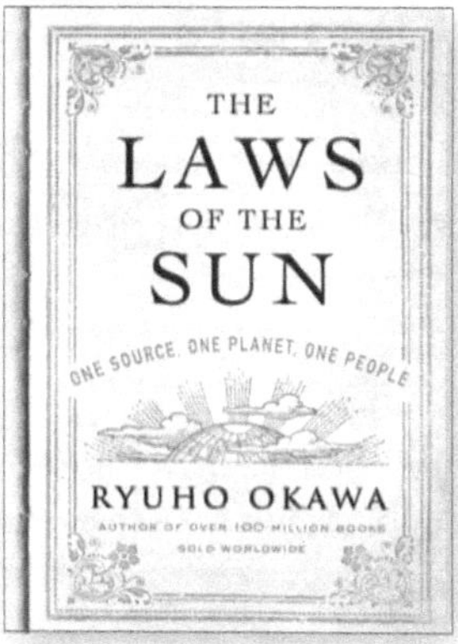

THE LAWS OF THE SUN

ONE SOURCE, ONE PLANET, ONE PEOPLE

Paperback • 288 pages • $15.95
ISBN: 978-1-942125-43-3

IMAGINE IF YOU COULD ASK GOD why He created this world and what spiritual laws He used to shape us—and everything around us. If we could understand His designs and intentions, we could discover what our goals in life should be and whether our actions move us closer to those goals or farther away.

At a young age, a spiritual calling prompted Ryuho Okawa to outline what he innately understood to be universal truths for all humankind. In *The Laws of the Sun*, Okawa outlines these laws of the universe and provides a road map for living one's life with greater purpose and meaning.

In this powerful book, Ryuho Okawa reveals the transcendent nature of consciousness and the secrets of our multidimensional universe and our place in it. By understanding the different stages of love and following the Buddhist Eightfold Path, he believes we can speed up our eternal process of development. *The Laws of the Sun* shows the way to realize true happiness—a happiness that continues from this world through the other.

For a complete list of books, visit ***okawabooks.com***

THE GOLDEN LAWS

HISTORY THROUGH THE EYES OF THE ETERNAL BUDDHA

Paperback • 201 pages • $14.95
ISBN: 978-1-941779-81-1

Throughout history, Great Guiding Spirits of Light have been present on Earth in both the East and the West at crucial points in human history to further our spiritual development. *The Golden Laws* reveals how Divine Plan has been unfolding on Earth, and outlines 5,000 years of the secret history of humankind. Once we understand the true course of history, through past, present and into the future, we cannot help but become aware of the significance of our spiritual mission in the present age.

THE NINE DIMENSIONS

UNVEILING THE LAWS OF ETERNITY

Paperback • 168 pages • $15.95
ISBN: 978-0-982698-56-3

This book is a window into the mind of our loving God, who designed this world and the vast, wondrous world of our afterlife as a school with many levels through which our souls learn and grow. When the religions and cultures of the world discover the truth of their common spiritual origin, they will be inspired to accept their differences, come together under faith in God, and build an era of harmony and peaceful progress on Earth.

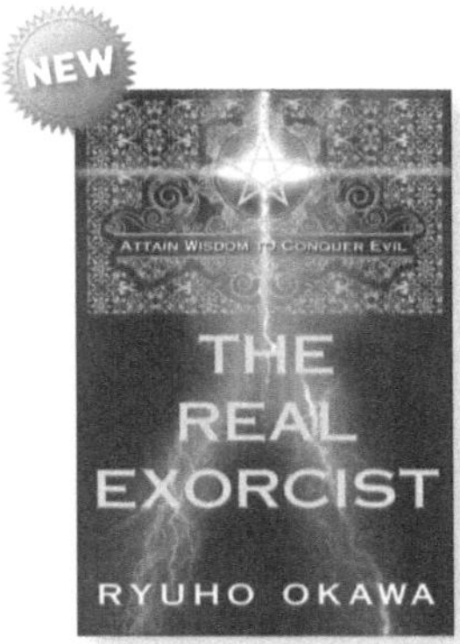

THE REAL EXORCIST

ATTAIN WISDOM TO CONQUER EVIL

Paperback • 208 pages • $16.95
ISBN:978-1-942125-67-9

This is a profound spiritual text backed by the author's nearly forty years of real-life experience with spiritual phenomena. In it, Okawa teaches how we may discern and overcome our negative tendencies, by acquiring the right knowledge, mindset and lifestyle.

THE LAWS OF STEEL

LIVING A LIFE OF RESILIENCE,
CONFIDENCE AND PROSPERITY

Paperback • 256 pages • $16.95
ISBN: 978-1-942125-65-5

This book is a compilation of six lectures that Ryuho Okawa gave in 2018 and 2019, each containing passionate messages for us to open a brighter future. This powerful and inspiring book will not only show us the ways to achieve true happiness and prosperity, but also the ways to solve many global issues we now face.

WORRY-FREE LIVING

LET GO OF STRESS AND
LIVE IN PEACE AND HAPPINESS

Hardcover • 192 pages • $16.95
ISBN: 978-1-942125-51-8

The wisdom Ryuho Okawa shares in this book about facing problems in human relationships, financial hardships, and other life's stresses will help you change how you look at and approach life's worries and problems for the better. Let this book be your guide to finding precious meaning in all your life's problems, gaining inner growth and practicing inner happiness and soul-growth.

---

*For a complete list of books, visit **okawabooks.com***

JESUS CHRIST'S ANSWERS TO THE CORONAVIRUS PANDEMIC

Paperback • 204 pages • $11.95
ISBN: 978-1-943869-81-7

In this book, the spirit of Jesus answers the causes, prospects, and coping strategies for the novel coronavirus pandemic. Instead of hoping for the development of an effective vaccine to come soon, we should use our spiritual power to defeat the evil thoughts that spiritually possess this virus. It's a book for all who believe in Jesus.

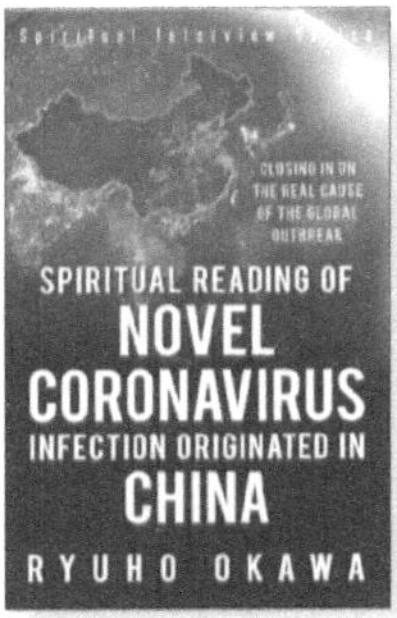

SPIRITUAL READING OF NOVEL CORONAVIRUS INFECTION ORIGINATED IN CHINA

CLOSING IN ON THE REAL CAUSE OF THE GLOBAL OUTBREAK

Paperback • 278 pages • $13.95
ISBN: 978-1-943869-77-0

This worldwide pandemic is not a mere act of nature nor a coincidence, but rather, heaven's warning to humanity, especially China. Through this book, you can find out "the immunity" against the novel coronavirus, among other shocking truths.

HEALING POWER

THE TRUE MECHANISM OF MIND AND ILLNESS

Paperback • 189 pages • $14.95
ISBN: 978-1-941779-96-5

This book clearly describes the relationship between the mind and illness, and provides you with hints to restore your mental and physical health. Cancer, heart disease, allergy, skin disease, dementia, psychiatric disorder, atopy... Many miracles of healing are happening!

THE NEW RESURRECTION
My Miraculous Story of Overcoming Illness and Death

THE ROYAL ROAD OF LIFE
Beginning Your Path of Inner Peace, Virtue, and a Life of Purpose

THE LAWS OF GREAT ENLIGHTENMENT
Always Walk with Buddha

I CAN
Discover Your Power Within

THE HELL YOU NEVER KNEW
And How to Avoid Going There

THE LAWS OF FAITH
One World Beyond Differences

THE STARTING POINT OF HAPPINESS
An Inspiring Guide to Positive Living with Faith, Love, and Courage

HEALING FROM WITHIN
Life-Changing Keys to Calm, Spiritual, and Healthy Living

SPIRITUAL WORLD 101
A Guide to a Spiritually Happy Life

For a complete list of books, visit ***okawabooks.com***

www.ingramcontent.com/pod-product-compliance
Lightning Source LLC
Chambersburg PA
CBHW030159100526
44592CB00009B/349
* 9 7 8 1 9 4 3 8 6 9 8 2 4 *